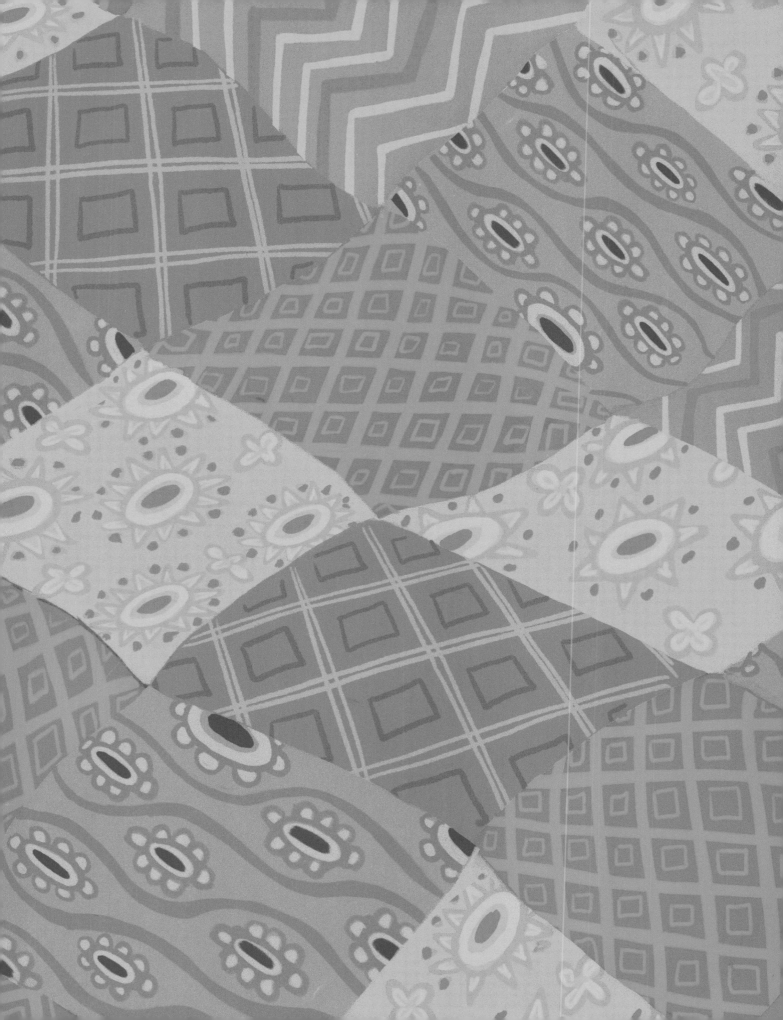

To Valerie, Yuvan and Noelle—
the most vibrant of colors in my Life!
—B.D.

Big Bold Beautiful World Media
Big, Bold, Beautiful World Media is a multimedia company dedicated to harnessing the power
of innovation and creativity to produce stories, experiences, and products that empower the
emotional intelligence of global generations.
gokulworld.com

Our books may be purchased in bulk for promotional, educational, or business use.
Please contact your local bookseller or the Big Bold Beautiful World Media
by email at gokulworld.com/contact

Hardcover ISBN: 978-1-7359606-0-9
Paperback ISBN: 978-1-7359606-1-6
eISBN: 978-1-7359606-2-3

Big Bold Beautiful World Media, 2021

Gokul Village and
The Mystery of the Vanishing Colors

Written by **Bal Das**

illustrated by **Beth Mills**

Gokul Village was a magical place, hidden in a faraway land. Whether it rained or shined, Gokul was always beautiful.

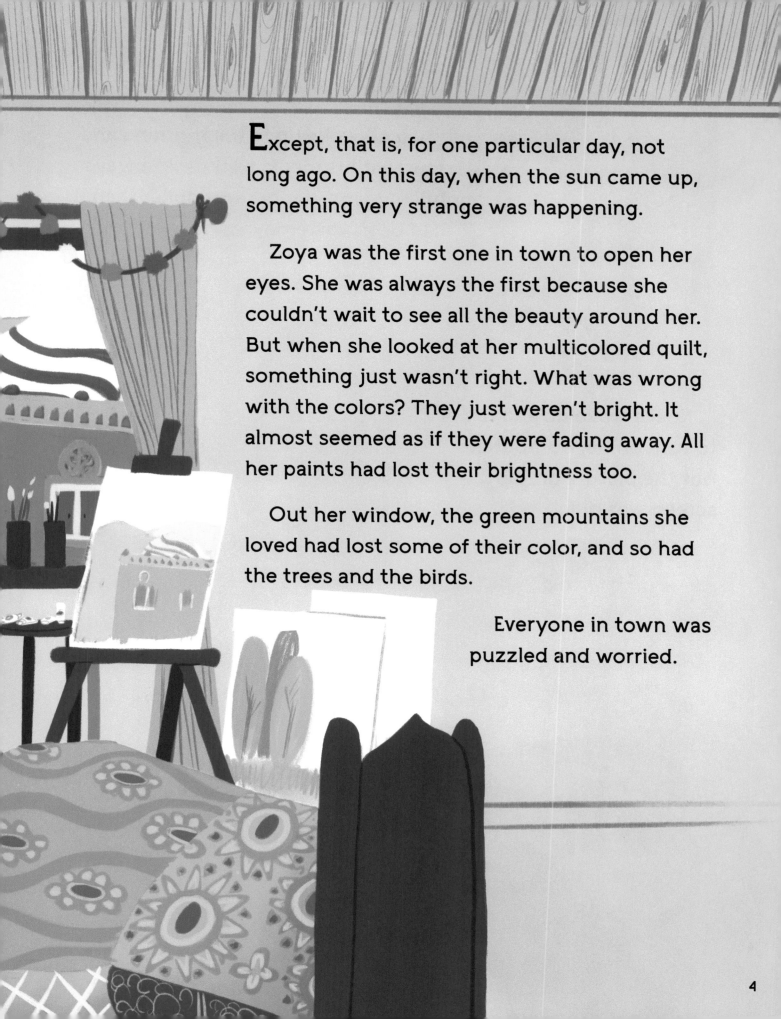

Except, that is, for one particular day, not long ago. On this day, when the sun came up, something very strange was happening.

Zoya was the first one in town to open her eyes. She was always the first because she couldn't wait to see all the beauty around her. But when she looked at her multicolored quilt, something just wasn't right. What was wrong with the colors? They just weren't bright. It almost seemed as if they were fading away. All her paints had lost their brightness too.

Out her window, the green mountains she loved had lost some of their color, and so had the trees and the birds.

Everyone in town was puzzled and worried.

The next day, things were a little worse.

Jacob woke up in the morning and saw that his magic backpack, always full of colorful food, was duller than it had been yesterday.

Noelle woke up and ran to turn on her computer. But the picture on the screen was dull.

Dalai's bike was dull.

Riya's kurta, waiting
to be put on, was dull.

And Christopher's
blueprint for a new
community center
was hardly blue
at all.

What was going on?

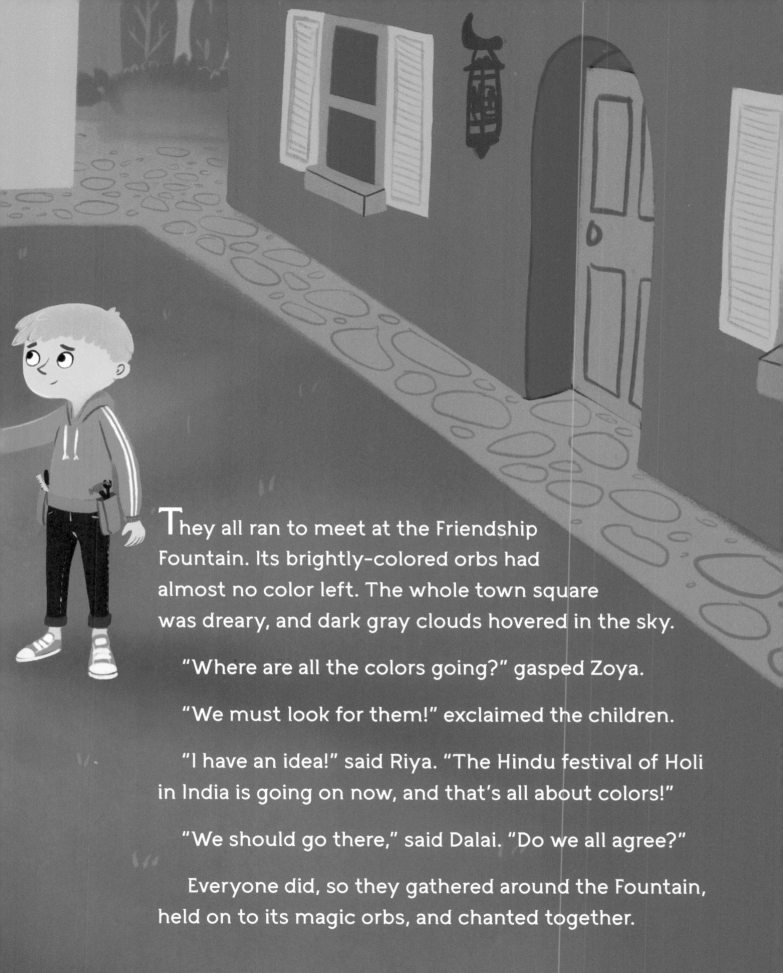

They all ran to meet at the Friendship Fountain. Its brightly-colored orbs had almost no color left. The whole town square was dreary, and dark gray clouds hovered in the sky.

"Where are all the colors going?" gasped Zoya.

"We must look for them!" exclaimed the children.

"I have an idea!" said Riya. "The Hindu festival of Holi in India is going on now, and that's all about colors!"

"We should go there," said Dalai. "Do we all agree?"

Everyone did, so they gathered around the Fountain, held on to its magic orbs, and chanted together.

"Waters of the world, connect us this day,
Waters of the world, take us away!"

And in no time, they were off to India!

But when they got there, a bad surprise was waiting. All the bright colors that should have been there were almost gone. Everybody there was sad. The children, the birds and the animals were sad—even the monkeys!

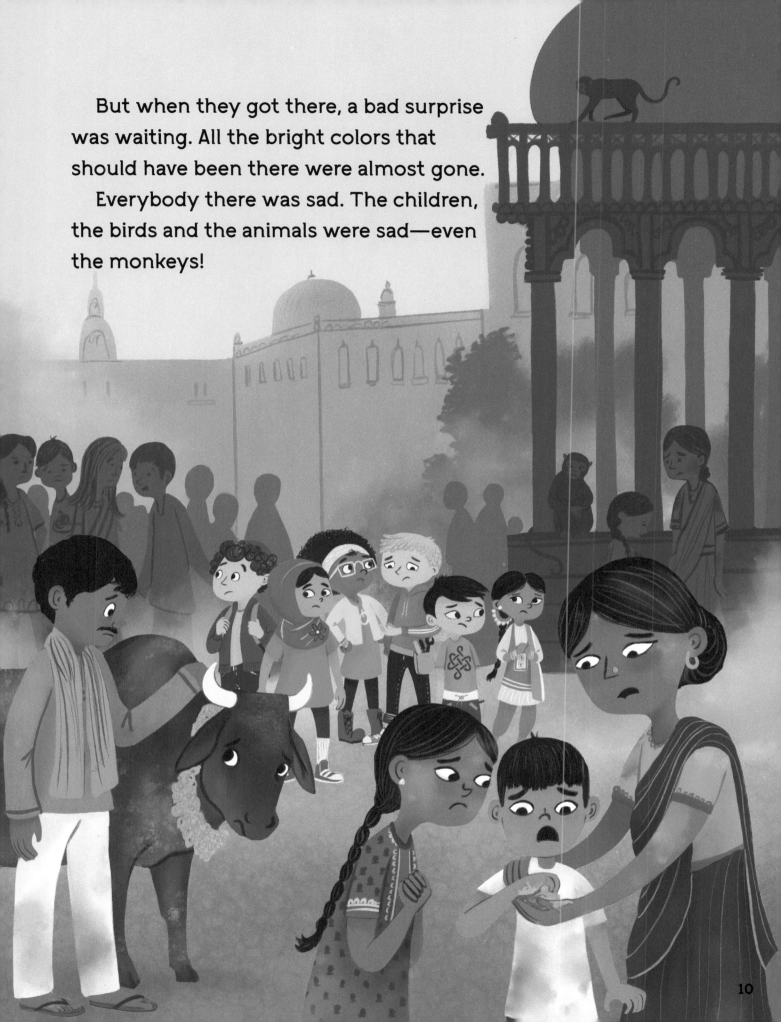

The children were stumped. Where had all the colors gone?

Jacob then spoke up. "You know," he said, "there is another holiday going on now, a Jewish one. It's called Purim. During Purim, children dress up in costumes and disguises. Maybe color is there in disguise! Let's go find out!"

And in no time, the children were off to Israel!

When they arrived in Jerusalem, it was another sad story. Lots of intricate costumes, but almost no colors!

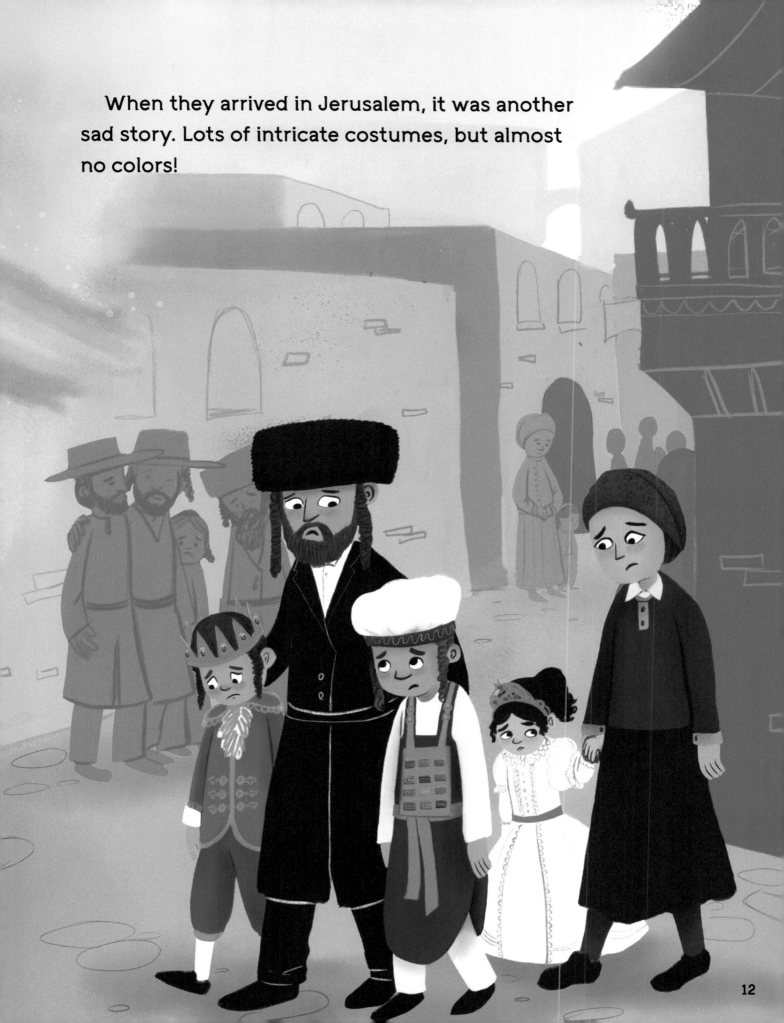

The children were out of ideas now. How could they live in a world without colors?

Then Riya spotted something strange. It was a group of funny little figures, huddled off to the side, all dressed in gray costumes. But what was that, poking out from under their costumes? It was color!

They ran over to the little group, their eyes wide.
"Could you be . . . all the missing colors?" asked Zoya.

"We are," said one of them sadly.
"But why are you hiding in gray clothes?" asked Zoya.

"**W**e felt like nobody appreciated us anymore," said Red.

"That's right," said Yellow. "So we decided we would just make ourselves scarce for a while and see if anybody even missed us."

"And where better to do it than in a place where everybody is in disguise anyway?" said Blue.

"Why do you feel like nobody appreciates you?" asked Christopher.

"**E**veryone is so busy all the time now," said Green. "Nobody stops to see the vivid color of new grass, or look at the rainbow in drops of water when it rains, or appreciate the beautiful colors of the butterflies when they spread their wings."

"It's true," said Blue. "Nobody
even looks at flowers anymore."

"Oh, but we appreciate you so much!" said Christopher. "Maybe we don't remember to say it enough, but we are so grateful for all the colors in our lives!"

"Where would we be without colors?" said Dalai.

"What if the food was all gray?" said Jacob worriedly.

"How am I going to paint without colors?" exclaimed Zoya.

The colors looked at each other, smiling.
Then, one by one, they took off their disguises.

Around them, the Purim celebration burst into color.

The children danced and jumped in their costumes. Jacob handed out delicious *hamantaschen*— the three-cornered cookies that are eaten during Purim. They were filled with colorful jams and jellies.

"Will you take a quick trip with us?" Dalai asked the colors. "We really need you in India right now."

"Of course!" said the colors. And off they went to India with the children.

As soon as they arrived, the Holi festival burst into color. The air was filled with bright, colored powders and colored water. Children and adults everywhere were laughing and screaming with joy. It was wonderful!

Noelle had iDEA take pictures from above so they would remember these moments forever.

After they had fun for a while, it was time to go back home to Gokul Village. The colors, of course, came along.

The people of Gokul were so happy to get their colors back, they danced around the Friendship Fountain until late at night.

"We must never take the things we love for granted again!" said Noelle.

"Never!" agreed Christopher.

As she snuggled into bed that night, Zoya ran her fingers over her bright quilt. "Thank you, Colors," she whispered as she fell asleep.

That night, the children of Gokul Village
dreamed of magical colors all night.